A Giant-Sized Day

Written by Deb Eaton
Illustrated by Michele Noiset

Once upon a time, a giant named Clad
lived in his giant-sized house.

Clad liked to stay home. Everything there
was just his size. He had a giant-sized
glass. It was as big as a pail.

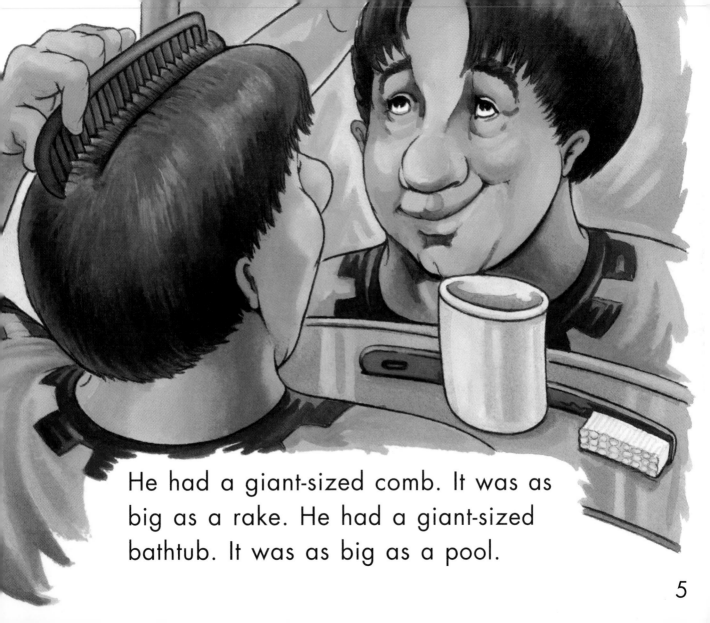

He had a giant-sized comb. It was as big as a rake. He had a giant-sized bathtub. It was as big as a pool.

Every day, Clad ate a giant-sized
breakfast. Then he took a nap.

6

When he woke up, he played a
giant-sized game. He ate a giant-sized
snack. Then he took a nap.

But one day, Clad was tired of taking naps. And he was tired of staying home. He wanted to try something new.

"I think I'll go to the beach," he thought.
"I want to play in the waves."

Clad took his hat, and off he went. He tried to take a bus to the beach. But the bus wasn't made for giants.

He tried to take a train to the beach.
But the train wasn't made for giants.

11

Clad tried to take a sailboat across the
lake to the beach.

But the sailboat wasn't made for giants.

Then Clad found a way to get to the
beach. He made giant-sized skates. He
had to put three skates on each foot.

The skates got him all the way to the beach. "Now I can play in the waves," thought Clad.

"But first I'll take a little nap."